Getting Value out of Agile Retrospectives

Retrospectives

A Toolbox of Retrospective Exercises

Luis Gonçalves and Ben Linders

Getting Value out of Agile Retrospectives

A Toolbox of Retrospective Exercises

Luis Gonçalves and Ben Linders

ISBN 978-1-304-78962-4 -9000

Tweet This Book!

Please help Luis Gonçalves and Ben Linders by spreading the word about this book on Twitter!

The suggested tweet for this book is:

New retrospective exercises: Getting Value out of Agile Retrospectives by @lgoncalves1979 & @BenLinders #RetroValue

The suggested hashtag for this book is #RetroValue.

Find out what other people are saying about the book by clicking on this link to search for this hashtag on Twitter:

https://twitter.com/search?q=#RetroValue

Contents

CONTENTS

Foreword

I started designing and leading retrospectives nearly two decades ago. I've been teaching others to lead retrospectives for at least a decade. I've seen how the disciplined practice of retrospectives can help a team. I've seen teams improve their practices, boost collaboration, and make better products. Retrospectives can help teams grow into empowerment. They can catalyze the process of change for a whole organization.

I've also heard tales of retrospectives that fail to bring change. Sometimes, these failed retrospectives have fallen into a rut. The team repeats the same activities in the same order over and over again. Their habitual practice doesn't spark creativity or new thinking. Other retrospectives fail because they don't allow enough time for robust exploration.

Effective retrospectives help teams short-circuit ingrained patterns of thinking. They broaden each team member's perspective, and help teams think, learn, decide, and act together.

In this book, Luis and Ben share the potential for retrospectives. Their advice comes from practical knowledge. They've learned how to prepare an organization for retrospectives and how to introduce them into an organization. They've done the work of helping teams choose and make sustainable incremental improvements. They've grappled with the pitfalls of teams falling back into habitual thinking.

Ben and Luis offer guidance to help you and your teams make the most of your retrospectives. They have collected activities that will help you and your teams think together and spark discussion.

In this pocket book, teams and retrospective leaders have a new and solid source to keep retrospectives fresh, focused, and full of learning.

Esther Derby
Co-author of *Agile Retrospectives: Making Good Teams Great*
Duluth, MN
November 2013

Preface

We are both active bloggers at www.benlinders.com and lms-goncalves.com. On our blogs we share our experiences on several agile and lean topics including retrospectives.

Blogging is one way in which we share our knowledge, and it's a rewarding one. We like the comments we receive on our blogs when people share their own experiences, and we love hearing from people who have tried the things that we write about.

Many readers have told us that they value our blog posts. We started thinking about how we could make things easier for them, by providing a small book on a specific topic - a book that they can carry with them that has hands-on information that they can use in their daily work. These thoughts led us to produce this book about agile retrospectives.

We are aiming this book at agile coaches, Scrum masters, project managers, product managers, and facilitators who have at least some experience with doing retrospectives. They know about the purpose of retrospectives, how they fit into agile, and how to arrange and perform them.

During the years, we have conducted many different kinds of retrospectives. We think that it helps when you develop your own personal toolbox with retrospective exercises. We have given this book a personal touch by including our own experiences which are marked with our initials *(BL)* or *(LG)*.

We want to thank the many reviewers of our book for investing their time and suggesting improvements: Robert Boyd, Paul van den Broek, Jens Broos, Gerard Chiva, Iñigo Contreras, Hans Dekkers, George Dinwiddie, Stuart Donaldson, Jos Duising, Doralin Duta,

Jutta Eckstein, Murrae-Ann Erfmann, Earl Everet, Gerald Fiesser, Don Gray, Linda Halko, Shane Hastie, Joy Kelsey, Gert van de Krol, Cem Kulac, Diana Larsen, Kjell Lauren, Niels Malotaux, Claus Malten, Paul Marsh, Oluf Nissen, Lawrence Nyveen, Pierre Pauvel, Kim Payne, Sylvie R., Sebastian Radics. Whitney Rogers, Cherie Silas, Hubert Smits, Lene Søndergaard Nielsen, Ram Srinivasan, Johannes Thönes, Asheesh Vashisht, Matt Verhaegh, Patrick Verheij, Dan Verweij, Robert Weidinger, and Willy Wijnands. Your feedback has helped us to make this a better book.

Having a foreword by Esther Derby makes us feel very honored. With us, many have learned the why and how of retrospectives from the book *Agile Retrospectives: Making Good Teams Great* that Esther wrote together with Diana Larsen.

We thank InfoQ for publishing this as mini-book. This helps us to reach a worldwide audience of passionate professionals involved in the adoption of agile.

Finally we would like to thank all the people who invest their time to read and comment on our blogs. Your feedback helps us increase our understanding of the subjects that we write about and makes it worthwhile for us to keep blogging!

Second Edition

After publishing the first edition as an eBook in December 2013 much happened. Many people downloaded the book and have been using it to do valuable retrospectives with their teams. In 5 months we reached 1000 readers on Leanpub and many more on InfoQ.

We received positive book reviews on Goodreads and many emails, tweets, LinkedIn comments and other feedback from our readers. It feels really good when people like your book and tell you what they got out of it. Thanks!

Readers have asked questions, pointed out mistakes in the book and sent us suggestions for improving the book. For the second edition we have fully revised the text based on the feedback that we go from them. This has improved the book's readability and usability. We thank everybody who invested time and energy to help us to further improve the quality of our book!

We started getting requests for editions of the book in other languages. To support that, volunteer teams in different countries are translating our book into many languages. The retrospective books in local languages are distributed via Leanpub. A big thanks to all the translators, reviewers, and editors: you are helping us to make our dream to help teams all around the world to do valuable retrospectives come true!

The second edition is the first version that is also published in print via Lulu. The handy pocket format is easy to carry whenever you are doing retrospectives or preparing them. We thank the InfoQ staff for all their support while preparing our book for print. Since the content is the same you can use the print and eBook editions next to each other. You can download the eBook at InfoQ and Leanpub.

When we started this, we didn't expect it to become so big in such a short time. Of course, this makes us very happy. We also think it confirms that retrospectives are important in agile. Every day, we hear about agile teams around the world that are regularly doing retrospectives. Our mission is to help as many teams as possible to get more value out of agile retrospectives.

If at any time you want to know more about Valuable Agile Retrospectives, feel free to contact us. You can also subscribe to our Valuable Agile Retrospectives mailing list (URL: eepurl.com/Mem7H) to stay up to date.

Ben Linders and Luis Gonçalves

Introduction

This book contains many exercises that you can use to facilitate retrospectives, supported with the "what" and "why" of retrospectives, the business value and benefits that they can bring you, and advice for introducing and improving retrospectives.

Agile retrospectives are a great way to continuously improve the way of working. Getting feasible actions out of a retrospective and getting them done helps teams to learn and improve. We hope that this book helps you and your teams to conduct retrospectives effectively and efficiently to reflect upon your ways of working, and continuously improve them!

This book starts with two chapters that provide answers to the questions What Is an Agile Retrospective? and Why Do We Do Retrospectives? These answers help you to understand the purpose of retrospectives and to motivate people to do them.

The chapter Business Value of Agile Retrospectives explains why organizations should invest in retrospectives and what they can do to get more business value out of them.

The Retrospective Pre-Requirements chapter describes how you can prepare your organization for doing retrospectives and discusses the skills that retrospectives facilitators need to have.

The chapter Designing a Retrospective explains why you need different exercises for retrospectives, how you can design a retrospective that is valuable for a team given their situation, and what you can do to develop your own toolbox of exercises.

The main part of this book is the chapter with many practical Retrospective Exercises that you can use to lead retrospectives with your teams. Any time you are running a retrospective and you do not know what exercise to use you can pick one of the many exercises from this chapter.

The chapter Benefits of Retrospectives gives you ideas about what agile teams can expect to get out of doing them.

Adopting Agile Retrospectives describes what you can do to introduce retrospectives in your organization and how you can improve the way that you do them.

In the chapter A Retrospectives Book in Your Language we have listed the different language editions of this book that are available to help teams all around the world to do valuable agile retrospectives.

The last chapter provides useful information if you want to stay up to date on doing Valuable Agile Retrospectives.

Getting Value out of Agile Retrospectives doesn't intend to teach you the theory behind retrospectives. For that purpose there are books like *Agile Retrospectives* from Esther Derby and Diana Larsen and *Project Retrospectives* from Norman Kerth (see the Bibliography for a full list of books and links).

With plenty of exercises for your personal retrospective toolbox, this book will help you to become more proficient in doing retrospectives and to get more out of them.

What Is an Agile Retrospective?

The agile manifesto proposes that a "team reflects on how to become more effective". Agile retrospectives can be used by teams to inspect and adapt their way of working.

At the end of an iteration typically two meetings are held: the sprint review (or demo) that focuses on getting product feedback and discussing how to proceed and the retrospective that focuses on the team and the processes that are used to deliver software. The goal of retrospectives is helping teams to continuously improve their way of working. This book is about performing and improving retrospectives.

An agile retrospective, or sprint retrospective as Scrum calls it, is a practice used by teams to reflect on their way of working and to become continuously better at what they do.

The twelfth agile principle states:

> At regular intervals, the team reflects on how to become more effective, then tunes and adjusts its behavior accordingly.

All team members attend the retrospective meeting where they "inspect" how the iteration has gone and decide what to improve and how they want to "adapt" their way of working and behavior. Retrospectives are an effective way to move toward short-cycled improvement.

The retrospective facilitator (often the Scrum master) should have a toolbox of possible retrospective exercises and should be able to pick the most effective one given the situation at hand.

Typically a retrospective meeting starts by checking the status of the actions from the previous retrospective to see if they are finished, and to take action if they are not finished and still needed. The actions coming out of a retrospective are communicated and performed in the next iteration.

To ensure that actions from a retrospective are done they can for instance be added to the product backlog as user stories, brought into the planning game and put on the planning board so that they remain visible to the team.

Why Do We Do Retrospectives?

Organizations need to improve to stay in business and keep delivering value. Classical organizational improvement using (large) programs takes too long and is often inefficient and ineffective. We need to uncover better ways to improve and retrospectives can provide the solution.

Insanity, it's said, is doing the same things and expecting different results. If you want to deliver more value to your customers, you have to change the way that you do your work. That is why many agile teams use retrospectives: to help them solve problems and improve themselves!

What makes retrospectives different from traditional improvement programs? It's the benefits that teams can get from doing them. The team owns the agile retrospective. They can focus where they see the need to improve and solve those issues that hamper their progress. Agile retrospectives give the power to the team, where it belongs! When the team members feel empowered, there is more buy-in from the group to do the actions which leads to less resistance to the changes identified as necessary by the actions coming out of a retrospective.

Another benefit is that the team both agrees upon actions in a retrospective and carries them out. There is no handover; the team drives its own actions! They analyze what happened, define the actions, and team members follow up. They can involve the product owner and users in the improvement actions where needed, but the team remains in control of them. This way of having teams leading their own improvement journey is much more effective and also faster and cheaper than having actions handed over between the team and other people in the organization.

(BL) My experience is that many of a retrospective's findings have to do with how people collaborate and communicate in their daily work. Soft skills matter in IT; software developers and testers are human and do actually communicate. But like everyone else they sometimes have misunderstandings, can be unclear in their communication, or don't hear or miss things that have been said. You can use different retrospective exercises to explore team working and communication issues. Retrospectives can be used to establish and maintain teams and to help them become stronger. Coaching and mentoring helps team members see where things went wrong and to improve, and retrospectives provide valuable input.

These kinds of benefits explain why retrospectives are one of the success factors for using and benefitting from Scrum.

Business Value of Agile Retrospectives

Agile retrospectives help your teams learn and improve, and in effect increase their business value to their customers and the company. They can make your organization faster, more efficient and innovative.

A few things that you can do in retrospectives to raise business value are:

- Make the team aware that we look for actions that they can do - empower your teams. A benefit of retrospectives is that actions are defined and done by the team.
- Focus on learning and understanding instead of blame. You can use the prime directive to set a positive culture for improvement.
- Limit the number of issues and the action items that you investigate in retrospectives. It's better to have a few high-quality actions than many actions with a risk that they won't be done. Try to change only one thing at a time.
- Use the golden rules for agile process improvement to help teams work together in a smooth, efficient, and positive way while improving the way they work.
- Focus on clearly defined problems and help teams to find improvement actions that matter to them and enable them to do their work better. Use retrospectives to give power to your teams and to empower your professionals.
- Use root cause analysis to find the causes (not symptoms) of problems. Then define actions to prevent them from recurring. When people understand the problems and their causes they are often more motivated to work on them.

- Follow up on and evaluate the progress of actions to help the team to understand why some actions worked and some didn't (double-loop learning) and make the progress visible.
- Use different exercises in retrospectives depending on the issues at hand, the mindset of the team, etc. Make sure that you have a toolbox of retrospective techniques. When in doubt over what to do, try something new!

If retrospectives are done frequently, where each one analyzes what happened in the iteration and defines actions to improve, then they will lead to continuous improvement with considerable business value in the long run

Pre-Requirements for Retrospectives

In *Agile Coaching*, Rachel Davies and Liz Sedley explore how retrospectives provide a way to engage with team members by improving their processes in direct response to problems they face. Unfortunately, it is common to meet teams that have already tried retrospectives and have given up. So where is the problem? Successful retrospectives need several items to be present and this is the topic we want to tackle.

In *Project Retrospectives*, Norman Kerth discusses five important prerequisites for a successful retrospective: "the need for the ritual"; "naming the process"; "prime directive for a retrospective"; "the darker side of the retrospectives"; and the "retrospective facilitator".

The need for ritual

Usually humans do not stop to reflect during projects. This is not a natural activity, which is why it's so important to formalize a behavior and make it a ritual. Rituals bring people together, allowing them to focus on what is important and to acknowledge significant events or accomplishments. It is extremely important not to use a retrospective to identify purely negative parts of a project. Every project offers positive outcomes and these should be celebrated like any other small victory.

Everyone that is involved in a project should be involved in the retrospective. A retrospective's huge potential for learning should not be off-limits to any team member. Another reason why everyone should attend is the fact that everyone views issues in different ways. This contribution is extremely important in designing better approaches for the future.

Naming the process

In our industry, retrospectives take many different names like: postmortem, post partum, post-engagement redress, etc. In agile software development, "retrospective" is the current popular name. It is important to name the process in a clear way so that everyone inside and outside the process understands it. Usually a team knows what it means but it is not uncommon for top management to misunderstand what is going on. "Retrospective" is a simple and explanatory word.

Prime directive for a retrospective

One of the basic ingredients for a successful retrospective is the "safeness factor". People must feel comfortable enough to share their problems, opinions and concerns. It is common for team members to realize that things did not go as smoothly as planned, and when this happens they must feel comfortable enough to speak up and suggest different ways to approach the problem. Norman explains some techniques to create a safe environment within teams in his book. Additionally, he explains that before starting a retrospective, we should communicate a prime directive: "Regardless of what we discover, we must understand and truly believe that everyone does the best job he or she could, given what was known at the time, his or her skills and abilities, the resources available, and the situation at hand."

We personally have used this idea several times and can guarantee that it works.

Avoiding the dark side of retrospectives

We have seen several retrospectives transform into complaint sessions. It is common when a retrospective is not well facilitated. It is important to understand the reasons for complaints and this can reveal a lot of problems, but if a complaint session goes out of control it can ruin the full retrospective.

People do not complain with bad intentions. They simply exteriorize what is affecting them. They have needs that are not being fulfilled and they need to express their emotions. Problems occur when the receiver is put off by the complaint and immediately enters defensive mode and counterattacks. This can end up in a non-productive retrospective. If all retrospectives end this way, people start to see retrospectives as useless and they will stop attending them.

One technique that we use is to request that people express their thoughts as wishes instead of accusations. This changes the tone of voice and creates a safe environment – and having a safe environment is one of the most important things for a successful retrospective.

The retrospective facilitator

All previous topics are extremely important, but without a good facilitator, a retrospective most likely will be a disaster. Becoming a good facilitator requires experience, training and a lot of self-study. Before starting a retrospective, the facilitator should have a clear idea about what he/she wants to get out of that session. An experienced facilitator will be able to do that, but less experienced facilitators may require help from more experienced facilitators. Each retrospective tackles different problems. The trick is to find the right exercises to solve the right problems.

Less experienced facilitators should start with small projects where people have known each other for some time and have already worked together. Another good option for new facilitators is to pair or apprentice with a more experienced facilitator. The junior facilitator can learn under the tutelage of the mature leader in real time. With experience, people can consider larger problems and larger teams. Becoming a good facilitator takes time and effort. Do not rush it or you risk an unwelcome outcome.

Designing a Retrospective

As a retrospective facilitator, it's important to have a toolbox of retrospective exercises that you can use to design a retrospective. This toolbox helps you to facilitate retrospectives that deliver more benefits to the teams that you work with.

Why different retrospectives exercises?

Teams differ, and also the things that teams deal with can be different in each iteration. That is why there is no single retrospective exercise that always gives the best results. Before starting a retrospective, you need to think about which exercises would be most suitable.

The risk exists that teams get bored when they are always doing retrospectives in a similar way. A solution to this is to introduce variation using different retrospective exercises.

Selecting retrospective exercises

The purpose of selecting retrospective exercises is to design a retrospective meeting that delivers business value. Value comes from doing a retrospective that identifies the most important things that a team wants to work on to improve their process (By the way, a process is "the way we work around here".)

But what is most important? It can be the biggest, most current impediment your team has. You can do a root cause analysis to understand it and define effective actions. Maybe something is disrupting your team's atmosphere and they can't get a hold of it, in which case the one-word retrospective could help.

Or it could be finding the reason why the current iteration failed, or why it was such a big success. You could investigate how to use the strengths that your professionals already have to improve further.

Structure of a Retrospective

The book *Agile Retrospectives* from Esther Derby and Diana Larsen describes the activities of which a retrospective typically consists:

1. Set the stage.
2. Gather data.
3. Generate insights.
4. Decide what to do.
5. Close the retrospective.

You can use the retrospective exercises described in this book to design a retrospective comprising these activities. For instance, a one-word Retrospective or a constellation exercise can be used to set the stage, combined with a sailboat exercise or five times why exercise to gather data and generate insights. Exercises like a team assessment survey or strengths-based retrospective can help you to decide what to do.

Retrospectives are used to improve continuously, thereby helping your teams and the organization become more agile and lean. You can plan a retrospective meeting and think about the exercises that you want to use, but always be open to changing it on the spot whenever needed, which is why having a toolbox of exercises is important.

Develop your own toolbox!

Our advice to retrospective facilitators is to learn many different retrospective exercises. The best way to learn them is by doing them. Practice an exercise, reflect how it went, learn, and improve yourself. You may need a specific exercise one day, so make sure that you are prepared!

This book provides you many different retrospective exercises that you can use to design retrospectives.

Retrospective Exercises

Using different kinds of exercises helps you to get the most out of retrospectives. The following sections describe the exercises that you can use to do retrospectives.

The retrospective exercises described in this chapter are:

- An easy but powerful exercise is Asking Questions. There are many different questions that you can ask. The trick is to pick the ones that help the team gain insight into the main and urgent issues and identify improvement potential. Then, by asking more detailed questions, it allows the team to dive even deeper into the retrospective.
- The Starfish exercise is a variant of the "What went well? What did not go so well? What can be improved?" exercise. It uses a circle with five areas to reflect on what activities the team should stop right away, what activities the team should continue with in a reduced role, what activities should be kept, what activities should play a bigger role in the future and what activities the team should start.
- The Sailboat exercise reminds the team of their goal, the product they need to deliver, the risks they might face, what is slowing them down and most importantly, what helps them deliver great software. It uses a metaphor of a boat, rocks, clouds and islands.
- When there are issues within a team that need to be discussed, you can do a One-Word Retrospective. You start by asking each team member to state how they feel about the past iteration in one word. These words are used to discuss topics that might otherwise not reach the surface.

- Team member can rate their performance as a team, by stating the Car Brand that they associate with the iteration. It allows everyone to share their opinions about the iteration and come up with topics that can be improved.
- The moods of team members are often affected by problems encountered while working together. Having team members state their feelings in a retrospective using the Happiness Index helps to identify possible improvements. This exercise uses a graphic representation of team members' emotions.
- If there are significant problems that a team wants to avoid in the future, you can use a Five Times Why exercise. This exercise uses root cause analysis to get to the deeper causes of problems and to define actions that address them.
- The Constellation exercise can be used to visualize if team members are in agreement or disagreement about relevant topics. It's an opener that can be used to help teams to feel comfortable and speak freely about any topic.
- The Team Assessment Survey allows teams to do introspection in different areas, for example: performance of the product owner, management of activities within the iteration, team spirit within the team, and implementation of technical good practices. This exercise is based on the team-assessment survey from the Scaled Agile Framework.
- A Strengths-Based Retrospective visualizes the strengths that your team members and teams have using a solution-focused approach. It helps to explore ways to use strengths as a solution to the problems that teams are facing.
- A High Performance Tree is a metaphor that is used to help teams draw a vision and define a destination where they want to go. At the same time it points out what needs to be in place for the teams to reach their vision. This exercise is based on the high performance-tree retrospective originally created by Lyssa Adkins.

- When teams have become more mature, Value Stream Mapping is an exercise that can help them understand their pitfalls and find ways to improve. The exercise visualizes the way that the team develops software. It reveals dependencies and shows waste within the software development process.
- When you have an agile project with multiple teams, you can do a Retrospective of Retrospectives to improve collaboration between teams. This is an effective way to share learning's across a project and to solve problems that a project is facing.

How are the exercises described?

All retrospective exercises are described in the following format:

- **What you can expect to get out of this exercise**: The potential results that this kind of retrospective can give you and the benefits of using this retrospective exercise.
- **When you would use this exercise**: Situations where this retrospective exercise can be most useful.
- **How to do it**: A detailed description of the exercise and how to apply it.

Asking Questions

One exercise often used in agile retrospectives is to ask questions of the team and collect and cluster the answers. The results can be used to define improvement actions that the team can do in the next iteration.

What you can expect to get out of this exercise

Asking questions helps teams that have just started to reflect and improve their way of working to become agile and lean. Realizing that they can get retrospective actions done motivates teams to learn and improve continuously.

You can help mature teams by asking more detailed and focused questions to help them to fine-tune their way of working.

When you would use this exercise

If you have never facilitated a retrospective before then asking questions is an easy way to start. Since questions can vary, it's also flexible which makes it suitable in many situations.

How to do it

With a team that is new to retrospectives you can use the four key questions that Norman Kerth defined:

- What did we do well, that if we don't discuss we might forget?
- What did we learn?
- What should we do differently next time?
- What still puzzles us?

The four retrospective questions are usually very effective. Asking "What should we do differently next time" urges team members to look for things that they want to change. It often helps to facilitate a discussion, to find out why a process needs to be changed and to build a shared understanding and commitment for the actions that the team will do.

"What did we do well?" is a solution-focused approach that can be used in a strength-based retrospective. The addition of "if we don't discuss we might forget" makes this question even stronger; if something good happened by accident, that's great, but what can you do to ensure that you will keep doing it?

The question "What still puzzles us?" can provide useful insights by revealing things that had previously remained unspoken. If things come up, a one-word retrospective can be used to deal with the team's emotions. Asking "What did we learn?" makes people aware that in order to become better, they will need to learn. If this question doesn't lead to answers in several consecutive retrospectives, it can be a signal that the team is not trying enough new things. That's something you can dig into using root cause analysis.

Asking questions is an exercise that is easy to learn, but the effectiveness depends on the questions that you ask to the team. *(BL)* Working with agile and non-agile teams, I have been doing project evaluations, audits, assessments using the CMMI and the People-CMM, retrospectives and many other kinds of feedback sessions. The questions below are a mix based on these frameworks, but worded in such a way that you can ask them in agile retrospectives to help teams to find things that they can improve.

Examples of questions:

- What helps you to be successful as a team?
- How did you do it?
- Where and when did it go wrong in this iteration?
- What do you expect, from whom?
- Which tools or techniques proved to be useful? Which did not?

- What is your biggest impediment?
- If you could change one thing, what would it be?
- What causes the problems that you had in this iteration?
- Are there things that you can do to these causes?
- What do you need from people outside the team to solve the problems?

The trick is to pick the questions that help the team to gain insight into the primary issues that they are having, and questions that help them to visualize their improvement potential.

Use open questions to elicit answers that provide more information, and use follow-up questions to help teams get insight into what happened. Ask for examples to make situations concrete, summarize answers to build a shared understanding in the team and come to actions that the team will do.

Starfish

The starfish exercise is an evolution of the typical three questions that are used for retrospectives: What went well? What did not go so well? What should be improved?

What you can expect to get out of this exercise

This exercise helps to identify problems of and opportunities for the team. Instead of the typical three questions, we have a circle with five words:

- *Stop* – These are activities that do not bring value to a team or customer activities that bring waste into the process.
- *Less* – These are activities that require a high level of effort and produce little benefit. They may also be activities that were brought into the team from the past but did not lead to any overall improvements to a process.
- *Keep* – Usually these are good activities or practices that team members want to keep. These activities are already being applied.
- *More* – Activities on which a team should focus and perform more often. For example, many teams tell me how pair programming is helpful yet they do not need to do it every time.
- *Start* – Activities or ideas that a team wants to bring into the game.

With this exercise, teams can get an overall picture of what's going on within the team, what is working and what is not. They can get an overview about failed as well as successful ones in the past. *(LG)* In my personal opinion, I think this is a great evolution of the typical three retrospective questions.

When you would use this exercise

I believe this simple technique does not require any special occasion. It might be interesting for situations when a team goes through several ups and downs during the iteration. This technique reveals good actions as well as less positive observations the team has performed and therefore might be a good tool for summarizing the iteration.

Starfish is suitable for any team. It does not require any specific level of maturity.

How to do it

This retrospective is simple to do. First, draw this picture:

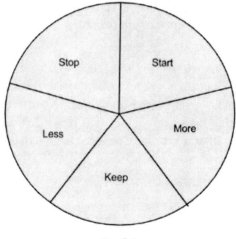

Starfish

One of the beauties of this exercise is the fact that a team need not be collocated. You can use tools like Lino, for example, to apply the exercise on non-collocated teams. Lino allows users to do everything needed in order to run this exercise.

After drawing the picture on a flip chart, it's good to start a brainstorming session by allowing the team to dump their ideas in the Stop area. After that, give two to three minutes to each person to read aloud the Stop ideas and spend 10 minutes on a short discussion to see if everyone is aligned.

Repeat the exercise for each of Less, Keep, and More.

For the Start part, add one extra step. Use the Toyota approach, choosing a single topic to discuss. You can hold a vote to see what the team considers the most important topic to start with. After selecting the topic, design a small strategy to make sure a topic is well implemented. This strategy might include responsible persons, due dates, and, most importantly, success criteria. In order to know if the implementation was successful, we must have a success criterion.

A theme that is chosen in the Start part does not need to be new to a team. It can be an improvement of something that is not working well.

The order of topics within the circle is important. *(LG)* I like to order them as Stop, Less, Keep, More, and finish with Start. I think this has a big impact. Starting with negative topics and progressing little by little towards the positive ones will help the team to end the retrospective with a much more positive feeling than if they did it in a random order.

Sailboat

The reason why this exercise is so interesting is the fact of allowing a team to think about their own objectives, impediments, risks, and good practices, in a simple piece of paper.

(LG) I learned this exercise a few years ago when I worked with Vasco Duarte. Recently, I saw an upgrade on Pedro Gustavo's blog where I got the idea of the rocks(risks). From my experience, this technique is well received by teams due to its simplicity.

What you can expect to get out of this exercise

This exercise helps teams to define a vision. It helps them to identify risks in their path and allows them to identify what slows them down and what actually helps them to achieve their objectives.

When you would use this exercise

This technique is simple and does not require any special occasion. It might be interesting for retrospectives conducted with more than one team. *(LG)* I had a situation, not long ago, when two teams worked together. Because of their level of dependency on each other, they decided to conduct a common retrospective to solve some ongoing issues. Using this exercise, we put the names of both teams on the boat and we reminded everyone that we are on the same vessel, heading in the same direction.

This technique reveals all good things and less positive things. It allows the team to identify possible risks and reminds them where they need to go as a team.

The boat exercise is suitable for any team. It does not require any specific level of maturity.

As with many other exercises, this exercise does not require colocation of the team.

How to do it

Draw a boat, rocks, clouds, and couple of islands as shown below:

Sail Boat

The islands represent the team's goals/vision. They work every day in order to reach these islands. The rocks represent the risks they might encounter along the way. The anchor on the boat is everything that slows them down on their journey. The clouds and the wind represent everything that helps them to reach their goal.

With the picture on the wall, write down the team visions or goals. Start a brainstorming session during which the team dumps their ideas into the different areas according to the picture. Give the team 10 minutes to write their ideas down on post its. Afterwards, give each person five minutes to read their ideas out loud.

At this point, discuss with the team how can they continue to practice what is written on the clouds/wind area. These are good ideas that help the team and they need to continue with them. Next, discuss how the team can mitigate the identified risks.

Finally, let the team choose the most important issue that is slowing them down. If there is disagreement within the team about which topic to tackle, you can use vote dots. At the end the team defines the steps to take in order to fix the problem and concludes the retrospective.

One-Word Retrospective

The one-word retrospective helps teams to deal with feelings. It represents a check-in where every team member summarizes in one word how they are feeling about the last iteration and the team. By discussing these single words the team agrees on the major problems that they are encountering and decides which actions they will take on to solve them.

What you can expect to get out of this exercise

This is an effective way for the team to discuss what is hampering them and come to an agreement on how to deal with issues. You can use this exercise to increase understanding and mutual respect in teams and improve collaboration. It can teach team members to express themselves better and find ways to deal with feelings, both positive and negative.

When you would you use this exercise

Use this exercise when there are sensitive issues within a team that need to be discussed. For instance when a team is struggling with the way that they collaborate or if conflicts and personal issues between team members are hampering the team spirit, this would be a good retrospective to conduct.

You can also do the one-word retrospective as a check-in exercise, to get the team members ready for a retrospective. If the team is having major problems, this one-word check-in and the discussion that follows may become the entire retrospective!

How to do it

Have each team member state how they feel about the past iteration in one word. Repeat each word, and write them all down on a flipchart visible to everybody. Then start asking why they feel that way. Use the exact words mentioned by team members to have a discussion in which the team members express feelings that otherwise would not reach the surface.

Work towards a shared understanding with the team and list the major issues. Next, check with the team members and identify if there is agreement. Ask the team what actions they plan to take in the next iteration to solve those problems.

A variant of this exercise is to use images from magazines or the web or to have team members draw an image to represent how they feel about how things are going in the team.

To be able to do a one-word retrospective you need to:

- Establish trust and openness.
- Respect people and their feelings.
- Be able to deal with the issues.

Trust is important in any retrospective, even more so when you are dealing with people's feelings and emotions. The team members need to feel safe to speak openly about issues and express how they feel. As a facilitator you have to make it clear that what is being said will remain within the team. It is up to the team to choose what they want to do with the results, even if they decide that they do not want to take action.

As a facilitator, you have to respect the opinions of the team members and ensure that they respect each other. If people start blaming or accusing each other, please remind them that the purpose of a retrospective is to understand what happened and learn from it. Remind them about the retrospective prime directive.

Finally, it's important to deal with issues that are brought up. People reach out and take risks by discussing them. They have to feel rewarded by the fact that the team does something with them. The team members have to leave the room feeling that they have been heard and understood. And they should feel that they have the strength to solve the issues together as a team.

Car Brand

One of the important parts of a successful retrospective is an interesting opener. We must set the stage, allowing a team to feel comfortable about speaking freely on any topic.

What you can expect to get out of this exercise

Even though this exercise is simple, it delivers a lot of information that you can use to run a full retrospective. It allows people to show how they feel about how the iteration went without deliberately expressing their opinion. This is especially important when the team is new to each other and the members are not yet comfortable openly expressing their feelings openly.

When you would use this exercise

This exercise does not require any special circumstances. It helps reveal individuals´ opinions, allowing everyone to have a common understanding of what the others think. This is important because team members must be aligned.

How to do it

When the retrospective starts, ask the team a simple question: "If you think about this iteration as a car brand, which brand would you choose?" You can explain, for example, that if the iteration went perfectly most probably everyone would choose a Ferrari. If the iteration had several ups and downs maybe a Fiat would be more suitable. Give them two or three minutes to think of an appropriate brand.

When you feel that everyone has had enough time to decide, invite them to reveal their car, one by one. Do not go into discussion at this point. People will have time to justify their choices later in the retrospective. Allow everyone to hear each member's choice first. This will provide an overall perspective on where the team stands. After this, give the team members 10 minutes to think about how they would change the past iteration in order to turn it into their dream car.

People will come up with dozens of changes, but experience tells us that a lot of them will be common problems. As facilitator you must try to classify them into the groups. Ask the team to use, for example, vote dots to select the most critical change they would like to see on the next iteration.

For this exercise, the topic was car brand but you can use anything that makes sense to you. Team members can be spread all over the world and are still able to run this exercise using virtual tools.

Happiness Index

Emotions are a crucial part of our daily life. Being able to connect emotions to events is a great way to understand what's going on around us. The happiness index is a combination of "Develop a Time Line" and "Emotions Seismograph" from Norman Kerth.

What you can expect to get out of this exercise

The purpose of this exercise is to draw a graphic representation of team members' emotions during iterations by connecting their emotions to events that happened in the iteration. With this kind of information, the team can identify what affects performance during the iteration. Knowing these direct causes can help a team solve future problems. For example, if the build server causes problems, the team will most likely become frustrated at the inability to proceed with the work and the general mood will drop. The team can analyze the problem and come up with solutions to tackle similar problems in the future. Similarly, if the team feels positive about a small victory, why not apply the same technique to succeed with similar issues in the future?

When you would use this exercise

This technique might be suitable for situations when a team experience many different emotions within the iteration and they wish to analyze the consequences. It's also a good exercise to use when the team has several challenges within the iteration and would like to understand better when and how the issues came about.

Happiness index is suitable for any team regardless of level of maturity.

How to do it

To perform this exercise, you simply need a sheet of white paper and some sticky notes. Draw two axis lines upon the sheet, marking the Y axis as positive and negative while the X axis marks number of days in your iteration.

There are two ways to do this exercise: within the retrospective itself with the whole team or in small increments throughout the iteration.

For the first option, create small groups of two or three people. Ask them to brainstorm about all the events that occurred during the iteration. Afterwards, ask them to graph the level of emotion with respect to the events of the iteration. When all groups are done, create a representation of all small groups on a single graph. Do not forget to put an explanation of each different emotion.

To execute the second option, each team member draws his own emotion level at the end of each workday. This approach makes sure that all events are covered and not forgotten.

Either way, the team will produce a fantastic picture of what happened during the sprint. With this kind of information, a facilitator can help the team to identify events that should be repeated and events that cause delay to the team. The root of problems can be found using normal root cause analysis techniques.

With a little imagination, this exercise can be applied to remote teams in addition to non-distributed teams.

Five Times Why

The five times why exercise uses root cause analysis to identify the deeper cause of a problem. It helps teams define actions that can eliminate those problems.

What you can expect to get out of this exercise

A five times why exercise helps to define effective actions to stop recurring problems and prevent similar problems in the future.

When you would use this exercise

When teams have repeating issues in their iterations and the retrospectives seem to be incapable of solving them, this exercise helps everyone get to the root causes of the problems.

How to do it

Repeatedly asking "Why?" builds a shared view of the causes. Each cause identified by asking why is questioned further to find out why it happened, until the lowest, root causes are found.

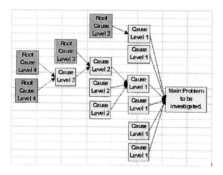

Cause and Effect Chart

Draw a cause-and-effect chart that shows on the different levels the causes found by asking why. Usually it takes four to seven levels of causes and effects to either reach a situation where nobody knows the answer or determine a stopping place where people feel that there is no need to dive deeper. At this point, you have determined a root cause! Repeat this until you have identified root causes for all higher-level causes that have been identified. Don't stop too early; make sure you really find the root causes.

Once you have all root causes identified, ask the team for actions that would prevent similar causes to lead to problems in the future.

There are some things to be aware of when using this exercise:

- Use real problems, not just imaginary cases. Ask team members to bring up causes that actually happened, not merely something that could have happened (this prevents assumptions). As a team you must recognize the causes and know that they are real to define effective actions and solutions.
- Know that there are always multiple causes for a problem. Don't stop when you have a first root cause. Invest enough time in analysis to find all of them, and get a good understanding of how the causes are related to each other.
- Vary how you ask why to better understand the real causes. This requires some skill from the person facilitating the retrospective. This can be your Scrum master (who might need mentoring on how to do a five times why retrospective) or an experienced facilitator who knows how the exercise can be used to get to the bottom of problems.
- Root causes almost always have to do with people. It's rarely a technical or tool problem. Most of the time, it has to do with skills, knowledge, the way the work is done, leadership, power, authority, communication, or collaboration.

The five times why exercise is similar to the Five Whys activity described in *Agile Retrospectives* by Esther Derby and Diana Larsen.

A five times why exercise is based upon root cause analysis of problems, a proven technique. Practical tools from root cause analysis that facilitators can use for this retrospective are a root cause analysis process and a root cause analysis checklist.

Constellation

To succeed with a retrospective, we must set a stage, allowing a team to feel comfortable to speak freely about any topic. The constellation exercise can accomplish this. To learn more about systemic constellations, you can visit this page.

What you can expect to get out of this exercise

This is an exercise for people who do not like or do not feel comfortable sharing their opinion/feelings openly. This is especially true at the beginning of a project when team members still do not completely trust every-one. Different cultural backgrounds and personality traits can make answering questions difficult. This exercise can help mitigate these issues because people do not need to speak in order to answer questions. Another advantage is that this exercise reveals what the whole team thinks about a certain topic without the need for early discussions.

When you would use this exercise

This exercise can open any retrospective. It might be suitable when the Scrum master/agile coach feels that the team does not have the same opinion about the practices applied within the team. This is a good exercise to reveal individuals' opinions, allowing a common understanding about what the others think. This is important because team members must be aligned. For example, if some team members think their level of automation is good but others do not, there is no way the team will work together to improve this topic.

How to do it

We begin a retrospective with welcoming team members and setting an affirmative goal for the session.

Start by making an open space. Move tables and chairs, if needed. Put an object on the floor and explain to the team that this object is the center of the universe. Kindly ask them to form a circle around it. Explain that you will read some statements, and that while you are reading, you would like them to move closer to or farther from the universe depending on how true the statement is for them. So, if they agree with the statement, they should move as close as possible to the center of the universe. If they do not agree with it, they should step away from the center. Once you read a question, let the team observe the system. As Lyssa wrote, "Let the system reveal itself."

You can choose statements within different areas that might need improvement – i.e. technical, innovation, and people areas. In the technical area, you can ask questions like, "How difficult is it to move to a scenario where we could release with every check in? How difficult is it to move to 100% test coverage? How difficult is it to completely get rid of manual testing?"

About people areas, you can state, "Working in this team gives me a fantastic feeling of reward. Working in this team makes me feel super appreciated. Working in this team allows me to develop myself as a person and as a professional."

Innovation statements can include, "I feel that we are the most innovative team in whole company. I feel that we have the space necessary to develop all our ideas. I feel that our product is so innovative that no one in the market is even close to having something like it."

Just choose a topic, ask several questions related to it, and let the team see where they stand. They do not need to speak at all; they answer with the movements that show their position in the system.

You can keep asking questions until you feel a good vibe from the team. To benefit fully from this exercise, at the end ask the team "Are you surprised with the shape?" Let them talk to each other a bit. It's important to allow healthy discussions.

As a next step, you can, pick the three statements with the most differing opinions for discussion within the team in order to bring everyone to a common understanding of where they are and where they would like to be. After that, just agree with the team who will take responsibility on different topics and close the retrospective. You can perform this exercise virtually. Having everyone in the same room helps, but it's not necessary. You can use tools like Lino to use with distributed teams.

Team Assessment Survey

(LG) During the last months, Dean Leffingwell has exposed the SAFe framework to me. The framework provides a team assessment survey.

This exercise provides a set of measures a team can use to objectively determine their performance at the project level.

What you can expect to get out of this exercise

The exercise helps teams on their agile journey. It allows teams to analyze how they are performing in different areas and identify possible improvements in the near future.

The assessment has four main areas:

- Product-ownership health: how the product owner is performing.
- Iteration health: how activities within the iteration are being managed.
- Team health: the health of team spirit within the team.
- Technical health: how well the team has implemented technical good practices.

Each of these areas has different questions that can be rated from zero to five (where zero is the lowest health), allowing the team to assess the areas that need more attention.

This exercise helps you to reveal the overall agile health of teams.

When you would use this exercise

This technique might be suitable for situations when a team wants to better understand how well they are implementing agile practices. This exercise will not solve specific problems that occurred during the iteration, but might reveal why those problems happened. For example, a team that finds a lot of bugs during development might learn that their unit testing or automation practices are not well implemented.

How to do it

To perform this exercise you use a spreadsheet with four main areas (product-ownership health, sprint health, team health, and technical health). For each area, create several statements that you think are appropriate. Have each member of your team answer these questions before the retrospective. You can use statements from the SAFe Team Scrum XP assessment that you can find in the Scaled Agile Framework. Listed below are two sample statements in each area.

Product-ownership health:

- Product owner facilitates user-story development, prioritization, and negotiation.
- Product owner collaborates proactively with product management and other stakeholders.

Iteration health:

- Team plans the iteration collaboratively, effectively and efficiently.
- Team always has clear iteration goals in support of PSI (potential shippable increment) objectives and commits to meeting them.

Team health:

- Team members are self-organized, respect each other, help each other to complete iteration goals, manage interdependencies and stay insync with each other.
- Stories are iterated through the iteration with multiple define-build-test cycles (For example the iteration is not water-falled).

Technical health:

- Automated acceptance tests and unit tests are part of story.
- DoD refactoring is always underway.

All these statements can be rated from zero (never) to five (always).

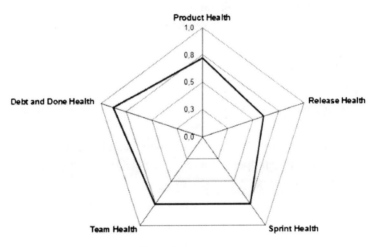

Team Assessment

During the retrospective, the team fills out the spreadsheet together and members evaluate themselves to see where they stand. If desired, you can create a graphic to display the result of the assessment. An example can be seen on the picture above.

Visualizing the assessment will let a team appreciate where they stand. With the graphic in front of them, they can decide which area they want to improve, choosing only one area at a time and one topic within the area.

Like many other exercises, this one does not require colocation of the team, as long as you have some kind of scoring and voting mechanism that everyone can access.

Strengths-Based Retrospective

How can you become an excellent team that is able to deliver and exceed customer expectations? By continuously becoming better in the things that you are great at. This can be accomplished using a strengths-based retrospective with solution focus.

What you can expect to get out of this exercise

This exercise helps teams improve themselves by focusing on their individual and team strengths and using those strengths to improve!

A solution focused retrospective is based on Solution Focused Therapy. This kind of therapy does not focus on the past but instead focuses on the present and future. It examines what works in a given situation, and uses that to address existing problems. It is a positive way of improving and exploring possibilities and revealing strengths that people and teams may not be aware of.

When you would use this exercise

In retrospectives, teams normally use an exercise to reflect on the work that they did, analyze what happened and why, and define improvement actions for the next iteration. These actions imply that they will change their way of working. A strengths-based retrospective is a different approach. Instead of coming up with a list of actions to start doing new things (which you might not be capable of doing), your actions result in doing more of the things that you are already doing and which you are good at.

If your team is working to improve their happiness, then a strengths-based retrospective can be used to identify what they are good at. Often these are the same things that make them happy.

How to do it

A strength-based retrospective consists of two steps: discovering strengths, then defining actions that use them. Both steps consist of retrospective questions that team members ask themselves.

Discovering strengths: Think of something that succeeded in this iteration that the team managed to accomplish beyond expectation, and which produced benefits for you, the team, and/or for your customers. Now ask yourself and your team the following questions:

- How did we do it? What did we do to make it successful?
- What helped us do it? Which expertise or skills made the difference? Which strengths that you possess made it possible?
- How did being part of a team help to realize it? What did team members do to help you? Which strengths does your team have?

The questions are based on Appreciative Inquiry, an approach that focuses on value and energy. These questions give visibility to good things that happened and explore the underlying strengths that made it possible.

If you are using the four key questions, the question "What did we do well?" can also be used as a solution-focused approach to find strengths that can be deployed to address problems a team is facing.

Defining actions: Think of a problem that you had in the past iteration, one that is likely to happen again. For example a problem that is keeping you and your team from delivering benefits for your customers? Now ask:

- How can you use your individual or team strengths to solve this problem?
- What would you do more frequently that would help prevent the problem from happening again?
- Which actions can you take, which you are already capable of?

Again, this applies appreciative inquiry by envisioning what can be done using the previously discovered strengths and giving energy to the team members to carry it out.

High Performance Tree

One big advantage of this exercise is its simplicity. This exercise is a fantastic tool that helps teams on their journey to become high performing teams.

The high performance tree was created by Lyssa Adkins. This exercise is explored in detail in her book *Coaching Agile Teams: A Companion for Scrum Masters, Agile Coaches and Project Managers in Transition.*

What you can expect to get out of this exercise

This exercise helps team to define a vision for themselves. Lyssa refers to metaphors as a core skill that is taught in professional coaching courses. This is exactly what the high performance tree is, a metaphor to help teams create a compelling vision. It's a way to create a path that leads to high performance teams. This exercise helps many teams find the next steps in order to achieve high performance.

When you would use this exercise

The exercise can be used in several different ways, and can be used by any team. However, the way it's used depends on the maturity of the team. We need to define the team's maturity level and adapt the exercise to that level. Lyssa states that in order for a team to be highly productive, it needs strong roots. When the roots are solid, the tree can flourish and bear beautiful fruit.

We mainly see this exercise used in three different ways:

- Team startup.
- A normal team that still has a lot of problems to solve.
- A good team that is looking for the next step to become a high-performing team.

How to do it

This exercise starts with the coach drawing a tree with the five Scrum values as the roots. This makes it also a great opportunity for the coach to teach or refresh the meaning of Scrum values. If the team is mature they can substitute their own values for the Scrum values. When the team is new and inexperienced, we recommend starting with the Scrum values.

Commitment is the state or quality of dedication to a cause, activity, etc. A commitment should never be broken - if it is broken, it was not a commitment but an empty promise and a lie. In the Scrum world, this means that everyone involved in developing a product is committed to working towards a common objective.

Courage is the ability to confront fear, pain, danger, uncertainty, and intimidation. In software development, these feelings will always be present and it is up to the team members to try to dispel anything that prevents them from being successful.

Openness is the ability to be open to new ideas, new approaches, and new ways of working. This is a fundamental state in agile software development because everyday teams encounter different problems that need to be approached differently. Being open is mandatory for success.

Focus is the process of selectively concentrating on one aspect of the environment while ignoring other things. In software development, this means teams should concentrate on one topic at a time. They should not start a new topic before finishing the previous one.

Respect is a feeling of deep admiration for someone or something elicited by their abilities, qualities, or achievements. In Scrum, all team members interact closely and respect is paramount for such relationships to work.

After explaining the Scrum values, you can list characteristics of high performance teams, for example: empowered, consensus-driven, self-organized, constructive disagreement, etc. These are some of the characteristics that Jean Tabaka refers on his book *Collaboration Explained.*

Explain that this combination will produce teams that can do anything, accomplish astonishing results, get the right business value, and get business value faster.

After this, you can engage the team in a healthy discussion to try to figure out what is missing and what is needed to allow them to advance to the next level.

New teams will learn how to become a high-performing team with this exercise. Established teams can revisit their performance and analyze what's required to become high-performing teams. Even teams that are already highly performing will find something they can improve upon in order to become better.

Like many other exercises, this exercise will have the most impact if all team members are in the same place but this is not mandatory. The exercise can be easily done using a web cam like Lyssa demonstrates on Youtube.

Value Stream Mapping

Value stream mapping is a lean manufacturing technique used to analyze and design the flow of materials and information required to bring a product or service to a consumer. Although value stream mapping is often associated with manufacturing, it is also used in logistics and supply chain, service related industries, healthcare, software development, product development, and administrative and office processes. At Toyota, where the technique originated, it is known as "material and information flow mapping". It can be applied to nearly any value chain.

What you can expect to get out of this exercise

Using this tool, you can visualize how your development process is working, allowing your team to identify several possible parts of the software development process that can be improved. This exercise will show how many dependencies and blockers the team has. Having this information available will help a team to decide how and where they can improve.

When you would use this exercise

This exercise will be more effective with mature teams. It reveals how the team and system interact. For this kind of exposure, the team must be mature. I believe if team members are new to agile they will not understand most of the things this exercise uncovers.

(LG) From my experience one of the most common things this exercise exposes is the QA/localization/documentation tail for each story. If the team is not mature enough they will not see this as a problem. I believe that most of the time only truly agile teams understand how important it is to reduce QA tail by introducing TDD, ATDD, and unit testing. Inexperienced teams do not realize how important is it to have documentation/localization done within the iteration. To get ideas on how to bring localization inside of the iteration see "Is localization delaying your release?". The value

stream mapping exercise will reveal some complex problems that only mature teams are ready to deal with.

How to do it

This activity is not an activity to perform during the retrospective. Instead, this is an activity to be executed during the iteration and then analyzed within the retrospective.

The easiest way to do this activity is to grab some flipchart paper and tape it to the wall. Then divide the space in equal intervals; each interval represents a day of the iteration. Draw a line on the Y axis; this line should be on the position Y=0. You should have a flip-chart for each story of the iteration. Collocation of the team is not required, you can just create an Excel sheet to produce the same effect.

During development, the team should be concentrated on one story at a time. If they are doing an activity that will bring value to a customer, each member draws a line on top of the Y-axis line. If they are waiting, blocked or doing some activity that does not bring value to the customer, draw a line under the Y-axis line. An example can be found below.

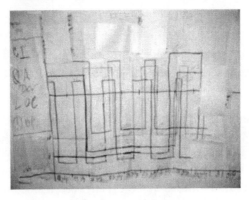

Value Stream Mapping

In the example above, you can see people responsible for development, quality assurance, documentation, and localization. The graph can be used to analyze the value and waste.

If you are new to this exercise, you can think of all tasks that are needed to accomplish a story as bringing value to customer. All other tasks result in waste. As it is used in the business world, customer value is the amount of benefit that a customer will get from a service or product, relative to its cost. Waste as Mary and Tom Poppendieck describes in their book *Lean Software Development* is:

- Anything that does not create value for a customer
- A part that is sitting around waiting to be used
- Making something that is not immediately needed
- Motion
- Transportation
- Waiting
- Any extra processing steps
- Defects

If a team is extremely mature you can start classifying all QA activities that are performed as validation versus part of development or bug fix, as waste. For example, unit testing, TDD, ATDD and other techniques can be considered QA activities if performed as a part of development. If we do testing at the end just to validate that everything is fine, then you can think this is a waste. Bug fixing can be considered a waste too.

The team needs to do this activity everyday in order to track all activities inside the team. Don't forget to write notes when people are blocked or in IDLE; these notes are important to be discussed in the retrospective. The possible result can be something as pictured above. The facilitator's job is to help the team to select the biggest problem, and help them to find ways to correct it. *(LG)* Like I said, I tried this activity several times and it's amazing how much information the team gets out of this exercise. For me this is one of the exercises from my toolbox that I most appreciate.

Retrospective of Retrospectives

Many agile projects have multiple teams who work on the same product. Each team can do their own retrospectives, and a retrospective of retrospectives can be used to share lessons learned.

What you can expect to get out of this exercise

Retrospective of retrospectives (RoR) help to improve collaboration between teams, and increase team contributions to a project. Use them to share lessons learned across a project, and to solve problems that a project is facing.

Since a RoR improves collaboration within the project, it can be a great way to handle risks and improve product quality. It can also increase the chances that the project delivers valuable functionality, quickly and continuously.

Distributed projects can also use RoRs to improve the interaction and working relationships of teams. In her book *Agile Software Development with Distributed Teams* Jutta Eckstein describes how you can organize project-wide retrospectives either as in person or as virtual meetings.

Corporate-wide improvement programs often fail, while retrospectives have proven to deliver continuous improvement on the work floor. RoRs enhance this by allowing teams to learn from other teams. It also encourages teams to team up where they see commonality. The sum is greater than the individual parts.

When you would use this exercise

A RoR lets you align the way work is done in a project over multiple teams. This can make things easier for people who work amongst all of the teams, like product owners, project managers and other stakeholders. A project manager will often participate in a RoR, as it helps him/her manage his project with agile teams. A RoR helps a project manager manage agile projects by stimulating collaboration and self-organization of teams.

You can do a RoR at the start of a project as this is when it is important to establish how the project will be organized, and how teams will work together. Another time to conduct it would be when a project is facing major repetitive problems that have to do with the way teams work together. You can get to the root causes of problems in a retrospective, which helps the teams define effective solutions.

This exercise describes how to use RoR in a project, but you can also do it in a department, or for the complete organization. Wherever you have collaborating teams, regularly doing a RoR can help you to remove barriers and keep things moving.

How to do it

In a RoR members from different teams come together to discuss reflections from their teams' retrospectives, and the actions that they have taken. Together they can decide on

- Additional actions that are needed.
- Re-prioritization of the teams' actions.
- How to work together doing the team actions.
- Improvements to the teams' actions.

A RoR can be done in many ways. You can define the topics to be discussed up front, which makes it easier for participants to prepare and focus. But you may also have participants suggest topics at the beginning of the RoR, where you will vote and prioritize directly. You can also use open-space technology to have people align on topics that they consider important.

We recommend doing a RoR after every (major) delivery. For most projects, that would be one RoR every three to six iterations, which means roughly every quarter-year. The idea is to do it when you have something worthwhile to look at, which is what has happened on the way to the last delivery. And you also have a goal for the RoR: what do we need to do to make the next delivery work better?

The outcome of the RoR goes back to the teams. It's the people in the different teams that are doing the actions. They are changing the way that they do their work (their process). It is up to the teams themselves to follow up on their actions.

What about team confidentially you might ask? Teams may have discussed issues in their retrospective that are private to the team. Is that something that is shared in a RoR? Normally not. *(BL)* The basic rule that I apply is "what happens in the team, stays in the team." Does that mean that you cannot discuss it in a RoR? Unless you can do it anonymously, without hurting individuals or the team, you cannot. But similar to the trust that is there within a team, there should also be a level of trust within the project. You have to be able to discuss things and assume that your words will not be misused by other participants.

Benefits of Retrospectives

Retrospectives bring benefits to agile teams. They help them improve and deliver value to their customers. And by improving team performance, retrospectives deliver value to your business.

Actions by the team, for the team

In retrospectives you look for improvement actions within the agile team that team members do themselves. Teams are self-organizing which means that they have the power to change the way they work (their process). If they want to try a different way of working, it's up to them to give feedback to each other, to discuss what happened, to learn, and to decide what to do.

The team defines the actions that they want to perform in the next iteration to overcome issues that they ran into during their last iteration, to work more efficiently and effectively, and to deliver more business value to their customers. Nobody can effectively change a self-organizing team but the team itself!

Product owners can be involved

If there are issues related to handling the backlog, doing planning, or dealing with the needs of the users, we recommend inviting the product owner to the retrospective. Team members and the product owner can together explore the issues, define actions to solve them, and improve collaboration.

In some cases you may also want to invite customers to the retrospective. For instance, it's helpful to involve them when there have been issues with the sprint review, when the team members and the product owner want to improve communication with the customers, or when you want to explore ways to involve customers more often into the development of the product.

Teams sometimes come up with actions to change the way they collaborate and communicate with current and future customers. Often times, they also want them to change the way they interact with the team, for instance to have them attend sprint reviews or how they provide feedback on the product. It is up to the customers to change their behavior if they discover that it would be more effective; it's not for the team to decide. Telling this to a team as a coach doesn't always make you popular but it's how it works. You can influence people but you cannot change them directly. People can only change themselves!

Team members can agree on how they will change, but individuals cannot dictate what others should do. Change triggers change, so let the action start within the team and watch how it influences others. Have patience: it usually works.

No handovers!

(BL) When I started with agile retrospectives, I discussed with my colleagues why we should do them. We already did project evaluations, so where do retrospectives differ and what would be the benefit of doing them? One difference is that agile retrospectives focus on the team, not on the organization. There are no handovers of improvement actions needed.

Project evaluations investigate what happened in the project, and recommend changes for the organization or future projects instead of defining actions for the current project. It's logical since most of the time a project evaluation occurs at the end of the project. But there's not much that can be changed in a project once it's completed. To accomplish the actions, the project team that did the evaluation must hand them over to another project team or other people responsible in the organization for improvement.

In an agile retrospective, there is no handover: The team members will analyze what happened, define the actions, and follow them up.

Buy-in from the people

You may remember a time when your company announced another improvement program. It would address the business's needs, and solve major problems that the company was facing. You probably wondered if it would solve your problems, and how it intended to do that.

Instead of waiting for improvement program to solve your problems, why not use agile retrospectives to take control of your own improvement journey? Solve the problems that hamper you and your team, the ones that you yourselves consider important to solve. One of the benefits of agile retrospectives is that they give you the power to do it!

Many large improvement programs fail, but not because of the people who manage them. These professions are usually capable and know how to manage change. And they have assured management commitment and funding. But what is often lacking is buy-in from the workforce, from the people in the projects and teams.

This is where retrospectives take a significantly different approach, as they are owned and done by the agile team. They decide where and how they change their own way of working, instead of having it dictated by improvement programs. Teams collaborate with managers and quality and process professionals to have changes that will last and are valuable.

Teams lead their own improvement journeys

Retrospectives empower the team to control their own destiny. A team uses them to solve problems that they consider to be the biggest hurdles. They can improve at their own pace, doing as little or as much as they consider possible.

Managers should enable and support teams in doing retrospectives. They can ask and expect teams to improve within the possibilities and constraints of the organization, and contribute to the organization's goals, but it is up to the team to choose how they improve and where they decide not to improve (now). A manager must respect the judgment of his/her employees and rely on the team's professionalism, trusting them to manage their own journey.

If a team needs professionals who are not part of their team to do their actions, like their manager or a support department then it is up to them to involve them. The team can, for instance, explain their needs, make clear what they expect and why it is important, and how the things that they request will help the team. A team should double-check their expectations: Is the request something that the manager or supporting department is able and willing to do? It is important to know what is feasible in the organization and to have that done, and prevent any false expectations.

Adopting Agile Retrospectives

This chapter describes how you can implement retrospectives in your organization. You may need support of an agile coach or consultant to back you in this.

Just as implementing any other agile practice, adopting retrospectives is an organizational change by which professionals adapt their way of working and behavior. If not properly supported, it may take a long time to establish or it may even fail.

To support teams in your organization in the adoption of agile retrospectives you can take the following steps:

- Make clear what the purpose is. Show why it's beneficial to undertake retrospectives.
- Have people that are capable of facilitating retrospectives.
- Start holding retrospectives, and frequently evaluate them.

Purpose of retrospectives

It helps if people understand why they should do retrospectives and what benefits they can expect, i.e. the value derived for the organization and for them personally (what's in it for me?).

How can you help those involved to understand why they should do retrospectives? Here are some suggestions:

- Discuss the need for continuous improvement to get results with agile.
- Make it clear that teams have both the authority and responsibility to decide how to do their work and to improve their way of working.
- Celebrate situations where things have changed successfully and reward success.
- Emphasize "why" over "how"; completing actions and getting results is what counts.

Capable retrospective facilitators

Doing retrospectives and carrying out the resulting actions takes time, so it's important to be both effective and efficient. Effectiveness is being capable of deciding on the few vital improvement actions. Efficiency is being able to find and implement the improvement actions quickly while keeping the invested effort as low as possible. Having retrospectives facilitated by capable people (Scrum masters or facilitators external to the team) with a toolbox of retrospective techniques ensures this.

Here's how to do this:

- Assign retrospective facilitators and/or qualify and authorize people as facilitators.
- Train facilitators in the purpose of retrospectives, and on the techniques and the skills needed for doing them.
- Mentor and coach retrospective facilitators (external coaches or self-coaching/mentoring).
- Share and discuss experiences with retrospectives.

The Retrospective Handbook by Patrick Kua provides practical information about how to prepare and facilitate retrospectives.

Doing retrospectives, and evaluating them

As with many agile practices you can learn retrospectives most effectively by doing them. Of course you need to prepare to do retrospectives by stating the purposes and establishing capable facilitators as mentioned earlier. Then start with retrospectives in your first iteration. Use a simple technique like asking questions or the sailboat exercise. Just start doing it with one or more teams.

When you finish your retrospective ask the people attending the meeting if it was useful. Did it help them to gain a shared understanding of how things are going? Do the actions coming out of the meeting make sense? Does meeting as a team to reflect feel good to them? These questions and the team's answers help you to keep retrospectives both effective and efficient.

Starting with retrospectives

(BL) I started by doing agile retrospectives in stealth mode. I didn't use the term retrospective but called it an evaluation. My reasoning for using retrospectives was to help my projects with frequent evaluations and improvement actions, thus reaping the benefits of the retrospective during the project and not having changes enforced on them.

Becoming agile is hard work and you may have to deal with resistance to change. Once you have become more agile things will get easier. When you have developed an agile culture and mindset, things will start to fall into place and decisions on dos and don'ts do often come easier. Frequently reflecting on your agile journey helps you stay agile.

Whatever way you choose to adopt retrospectives, ensure that you keep on doing them. Even if things seem to be going well, there are always ways to improve!

A Retrospectives Book in Your Language

This book is being translated to many languages with teams of volunteers in different countries. Many translators, reviewers and editors are helping us to make our dream come true: to help teams all around the world to do valuable agile retrospectives!

Why do we work with volunteers in translating our book? Because we can! People started asking us if they can help with the translation (just as people volunteered to review the English version). When we reached out to ask for help, people let us know that they would love act on it. We ask them if they know other people in their network, and they invite them to join the team. It works!

Translating for us is another way to share knowledge and experience with agile retrospectives. Our volunteer teams consist of highly motivated driven people. They want to know about retrospectives and this is a way for them to learn the retrospective exercises and use them in their daily work. As authors we support them by explaining the exercises, answering questions and sharing our knowledge and experience. If you want to work with us in a similar way feel free to contact us via luis.goncalves@oikosofy.com or BenLinders@gmail.com.

Getting Value out of Agile Retrospectives will be published in Español, Nederlands, Deutsch, Francais, Chinese, Japanese, Italiano, русский and Português

You can subscribe yourself to the books that are being translated on Leanpub to stay up to date and to become one of the first readers of this book about agile retrospectives in your language!

Valuable Agile Retrospectives

First of all, we want to thank you for reading our book. If you reached this point, it means you survived the experience of reading it :) We hope it was a good experience and that you have gained plenty of new ideas to apply in your next retrospectives.

This book is the beginning of a journey. We are growing a small ecosystem around this book and plan to release more exercises in the future, how-to´s, retrospectives advice, and many other things. If you want to stay up to date, the best way is to sub-scribe to our Valuable Agile Retrospectives mailing list - URL: eepurl.com/Mem7H.

We are offering a half year of our work to the community to help teams improve all over the world. In return, we ask you to help us spread the word: forward this book to your colleagues, friends, R&D organizations or anyone that could benefit from it. If you want to tweet about it, please use #RetroValue to spread the word.

We are always looking for feedback. Feel inspired to write a Goodreads review or contact us via luis.goncalves@oikosofy.com or BenLinders@gmail.com. We love to hear from you.

You can read our blogs: lmsgoncalves.com and www.benlinders.com. If you are too busy to visit blogs, we can send an email when we have news for you. Add yourself to our mailing-lists: Luis´s at (eepurl.com/JOTXL) and Ben's at (www.benlinders.com/subscribe/)

Now is time to say goodbye and wish you all the best.

Yours, Luis and Ben

Bibliography

Our Blogs

Welcome to the World of Luis Gonçalves - lmsgoncalves.com

Ben Linders - Sharing my Experience - www.benlinders.com

Books

Lyssa Adkins. *Coaching Agile Teams: A Companion for ScrumMasters, Agile Coaches, and Project Managers in Transition.* Addison-Wesley, 2010.

Rachel Davies and Liz Sedley. *Agile Coaching.* The Pragmatic Programmers, LLC, 2009.

Esther Derby and Diana Larsen. *Agile Retrospectives: Making Good Teams Great.* The Pragmatic Programmers, LLC, 2006.

Jutta Eckstein. *Agile Software Development with Distributed Teams.* Dorset House, 2010.

Norman Kerth. *Project Retrospectives: A Handbook for Team Reviews.* Dorset House, 2001.

Henrik Kniberg. *Scrum and XP from the Trenches.* InfoQ, 2007.

Patrick Kua. *The Retrospective Handbook: A guide for agile teams.* Leanpub, 2013.

Dean Leffingwell. *Scaling Software Agility: Best Practices for Large Enterprises.* Addison-Wesley, 2007.

Mary Poppendieck and Tom Poppendieck. *Lean Software Development: An Agile Toolkit.* Addison-Wesley, 2003.

Mike Rother. *Toyota Kata.* McGraw-Hill, 2009.

Jean Tabaka. *Collaboration Explained: Facilitation Skills for Software Project Leaders.* Addison-Wesley, 2006.

Links

Manifesto for Agile Software Development - agilemanifesto.org

retrospectives.eu

retrospectives.com

retrospectivewiki.org